Donna

Love matters
& you
do!

♡ Alina

I Am...

Daily Reflections to Uplift your Soul
and Connect You to Mother Earth

Alina R. Haitz

BALBOA
PRESS
A DIVISION OF HAY HOUSE

Interior Graphics/Art Credit:
--Each image has been cited accordingly.--

Balboa Press books may be ordered through booksellers or by contacting:

Balboa Press
A Division of Hay House
1663 Liberty Drive
Bloomington, IN 47403
www.balboapress.com
1 (877) 407-4847

Printed in the United States of America.

ISBN: 978-1-4525-1928-9 (sc)
ISBN: 978-1-4525-1929-6 (e)

Library of Congress Control Number: 2014913389

Balboa Press rev. date: 10/14/2014

Contents

Source: 3286zauber

I am the Sunflower

The Sunflower's large head is bright and circular and portrays the sun. The Sunflower represents vitality, warmth, nourishment, healing, and attaining unity with light.

I am the Sunflower. I bloom brightly. I seek the light, which is my connection with the Source of my own understanding, which I choose to call Mother Earth or Mother Nature. I naturally heal my physical and emotional wounds by allowing Mother Earth to care for me through the light of the sun, water from the rain, and the activity of all beings around me. The Sunflower appears bright and happy. I am grateful for my feelings of happiness.

I remember the Sunflower. With strength and beauty from the inside out, I stand free and am proud to be who I am today. No matter how many challenges or difficult situations are in my life, I maintain my peace within. I forgive myself and others. Forgiveness is a gift I give to myself. I embrace the warmth and light of the Sun in order to navigate through my life's journey.

TODAY:
I am strong inside and out. I love myself. I am supported.

Source: http://www.robotbyn.se/solsystemet/images/sun.jpg

I am the Sun

The Sun is one of the brightest stars and is considered
the center of humankind's existence. It is associated with
cosmic power, the mind, and intellect. The Sun is a symbol
for life, power, energy, self, strength, and force.

I am the Sun. Every morning I rise is a gift and an opportunity to
start anew. I can be as bright as the Sun, positive and grateful, or I can
choose to go back to bed, go under my covers, never to face the day.
If the Sun decided that it was too tired to rise, I would surely miss
its presence. I, too, would be missed if I did not rise each morning.

I remember the Sun. I am an important and dynamic contributor
to Mother Earth. I am loved and significant enough that I
awake to live each day. My feelings vary, just as the Sun's rays
are brighter some days, but I appreciate my flow of energy.
I glow brightly, radiating love and positive vibrations.

TODAY:
I am perfect just as I am. I love myself. I am a vital part of this world.

Source: Tiago Fioreze

I am the Ocean

———————

The Ocean comprises a large part of Mother Earth.
It symbolizes strength, domination, unpredictability,
calmness, hope, truth, and letting go of negativity.

I am the Ocean. The Ocean's beautiful waves brush up against
the sand and create a sense of calmness. Although the Ocean
is powerful and strong, it allows Mother Nature to step in:
the wind alters its currents and the sun varies its temperature.
I, too, experience many changes throughout my life but,
just as the Ocean, I do not resist or question these shifts. I
naturally adjust and accept the forces of Mother Nature.

I remember the Ocean. I am open to change and I embrace my
life's experiences and challenges. I am trusting of Mother Earth
but still powerful through my individual actions. I let go of the
concept of trying to control anything or anybody but myself.

TODAY:
I am peaceful and open to a new day. I love myself. I shift with life.

Source: Rob Young

I am the Oak Tree

—✳—

The Oak Tree is the king of the forest. It is balanced, courageous, strong, and supportive of life. Although the king, the Oak is often struck by lightning, leaving the trunk twisted and withered. Yet, the Oak still manages to survive for centuries.

I am the Oak Tree. I am grounded and the king of my world. I am truly the most important part of my life. I am the only one that I am with at all times. Just like the Oak Tree, though, I support other living beings. I listen, care, and have compassion. Other creatures and elements of Mother Earth rely on me. I realize I must rely on myself as well.

I remember the Oak Tree. I am wise and willing. I have a purpose in this world. Even if I am not sure of my purpose at this moment, I trust that it will be revealed in its own time frame, not mine.

TODAY:
I am grounded and wise. I love myself. I have
a purpose. I am king of my world.

Source:Friendlystar

I am a Star

Stars are light years away from planet Earth and many cannot be seen by the naked eye. Some Stars visibly stand out from the rest because the other stars are either too far away or obscured by clouds.

I am a Star. I shine brightly. Stars are not visible during the day, however, they are still in the sky. Just like the Stars, I am confident in my abilities, characteristics, and beauty. Even when Stars are not acknowledged because the sun is out, Stars do not feel neglected or less. They maintain themselves and know that eventually they will have their time to be recognized.

I remember the Stars. I am included and significant but also experience enjoyment and gratitude when others shine brightly. I accept my role as one of many Stars. I know who I am and feel confident in what I do, so I walk through the journey of life with positive thoughts and joyful feelings.

TODAY:
I accept myself. I love myself. I have meaning but also value others when they shine brightly.

Source: Mindaugas Urbonas

I am a Swan

The Swan is known as one of the most beautiful birds. It is referred to as the 'bird of light.' The Swan symbolizes tranquility, sensitivity, royalty, power, and love. Although the Swan is the largest water bird, it possesses the ability to fly great heights with grace and power.

I am a Swan. I am beautiful inside and out. The Swan's grace makes it attractive. Its beauty is not only external; its beauty lies within. It pauses, takes its time, and is not a greedy type searching for food scraps. The Swan discerns what to eat and eats only what it needs.

I remember the Swan. I am graceful and serene, powerful and yet peaceful. My beauty lies within; I see it in myself, others, and in each new day. I take only what I need. I am flexible, calm, and loving. I share my beauty with Mother Earth and receive it in return.

TODAY:

I am beautiful. I love myself. I am serenely filled with grace and love.

Source: Euro-t-guide.com

I am a Lion

—❦—

The Lion is king of the jungle and known to be courageous, strong, and noble. It sleeps and rests for most of the day and does not stress or get anxious about when or what it will be fed. The Lion trusts that the Lioness, its female partner, will hunt and provide while the Lion serves as a guard and protector of their cubs. The Lion is a distinctive leader and honorable warrior.

I am a Lion. I remain strong through challenges and stand tall when times are difficult or seem unfair. I understand that these hard times are part of the cycle of life with valuable lessons to be learned. I am seen as royalty to my Creator, just as the Lion is to those living in the jungle. I know in my heart that I must trust that my journey will work out exactly as it should. I allow the process to happen.

I remember the Lion. I am full of courage to work through my challenges. I am powerful, brave, and noble. I am a peaceful warrior and take pride in my distinctive nature. I feel connected to Mother Earth; I trust that everything will unfold in its own proper time.

TODAY:
I am noble. I love myself. I am brave because I trust.

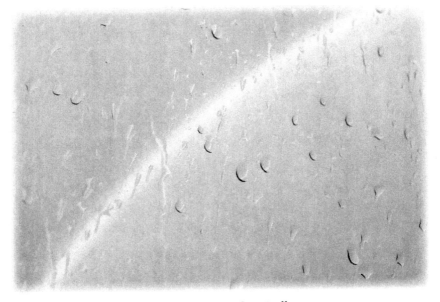

Source: Massimo Catarinella

I am the Rain

———◦◦◦◦◦———

The Rain serves Mother Earth. It is responsible for depositing most of the fresh water on Earth. Rain takes many forms, from light Rainfalls to monsoons and tropical cyclones. Rain is extremely important to our agriculture and too much or too little Rainfall can be destructive or devastating. The Rain is so vital to Mother Earth, but commonly considered a nuisance.

I am the Rain – not the inconvenient kind of Rain – but a server of Mother Earth. I am responsible so I carry out my duties as a human being. This includes connecting to my inner self and following my purpose in order to serve. If I do not feel connected to my purpose, I understand I still have one. I just need to open myself to its possibilities. Like dancing in the Rain, I have a sense of freedom.

I remember the Rain. The Rain is essential to Mother Earth for survival. As the Rain, I have cycles of droughts and floods, but I recognize how purposeful and vital I am to this planet. The Rain does not judge its purpose or productivity. I am non-judgmental of myself and others as well.

TODAY:
I serve a higher purpose. I love myself. I accept and appreciate my characteristics.

Source: Wouter-Hagens

I am a Turtle

—⁓⌒⊙⌒⊙⌒⊙⌒⁓—

Turtles are one of the longest living creatures of Mother Earth and one of the oldest reptiles. They have a hard protective shell surrounding them. Few living beings possess this protection. Turtles have sharpened senses. They are known for their slow and steady pace and patient, easy-going nature. Tranquil, wise, and secure, the Turtle cannot separate itself from its shell.

I am a Turtle. I am connected to Mother Earth just as the Turtle is to its shell. I am grateful for this body because of its protection and distinctiveness. Like the Turtle, I am persistent, stable, mindful of the present moment, and confident in my ability to complete daily tasks.

I remember the Turtle. I embrace my differences. I feel supported and nurtured by Mother Earth and I protect and value Her in return. I am connected, secure, and present.

TODAY:
I am patient and tranquil. I love myself. I feel a sense of peace by living in the present moment.

Source: Charlesjsharp

I am a Crab

—⁓◦◦◦⁓◦⁓◦⁓◦◦◦⁓—

The Crab is known for its unique forward and backward walking motion. As the Crab grows, it casts off its shell for a new one. The Crab also has a regenerative feature in which its claws and legs are restored if it experiences trauma. Usually associated with the human mood of being "Crabby," meaning snappy or irritable, the Crab is actually a symbol for transformation, renewal, and growth.

I am a Crab. My life's path is not always direct, which is similar to the Crab's walking patterns. However, I am open to less known alternatives and feel guided in my journey. I understand that I am supposed to be exactly where my feet are grounded at this moment. If I feel exhausted, anxious, or dull, I know I can be easily revived, restored, and reborn at any moment. I grow in my process of being.

I remember the Crab. I have the ability to make subtle shifts for positive changes in my life. I navigate through my journey aware that not all paths are direct or easy. When I am in crisis or going through a challenging time, I believe in the possibilities of transformation and restoration. Each day is an opportunity for renewal.

TODAY:
I am teachable. I love myself. I am restored.

Source: USDA.gov

I am a Pig

—⁓⁓⚬⚬⚬⚬⁓⁓—

Synonymous with several negative human attributes such as greed, gluttony, lack of cleanliness, and male chauvinism, the Pig is actually highly intelligent and social. The Pig has an excellent ability to hear and smell. As a pet, the Pig is independent and easy to train, unlike its household pet counterparts.

I am the Pig; I, too, am trainable. Although this may at first carry a negative connotation, I understand that this stigma has nothing to do with how I feel inside. The Pig does not care how other living beings categorize or describe him. The Pig intuitively knows its strengths and weaknesses and focuses on its positive and useful abilities. I am the Pig since I am also independent and do not need attention from others to feel validated.

I remember the Pig. I accept, approve of, and take pride in myself regardless of what others may think, feel, or say. The only approval I need is from my own self and Mother Earth. I was created exactly the way I was intended. I am useful and worthy.

TODAY:
I am independent and social. I love myself. I have a positive outlook.

Source: Mark Szczepanek

I am a Snake

———✦———

The Snake is legless yet still capable of moving on land and through water. It is commonly known for shedding its skin, which rids the Snake of parasites and creates a new, brighter, and larger layer of skin. Although associated with being deadly, dangerous, sneaky, and vindictive, the Snake also represents healing, cycles of rebirth, and is an insignia for the medical profession.

I am a Snake. I focus on my positive attributes and abilities. I embrace my weaknesses and flaws but do not allow them to impede my movement. As the Snake sheds its older skin, I also let go of my old ideas, limiting beliefs, and negative past experiences. In order to create room for my future goals, I release resentments, anger, self-centeredness and self-pity, and also forgive myself and others. Although this may be difficult, I take these healing actions and then feel cleansed and renewed.

I remember the Snake. I move forward through my life. To maintain serenity, vitality, and health, I release those characteristics, thoughts, and emotions that do not serve my mind, body, and spirit. I am balanced, happy, and whole. I continue this renewal daily as I practice self-love.

TODAY:
I am healthy. I love myself. I am worthy of renewal and change.

Source: JJ Harrison

I am a Seagull

———∾∾∘૯∿૭∘૯∾∘∿———

The Seagull is commonly recognized as an annoyance and one who steals food. However, the Seagull is resourceful, inquisitive, and intelligent. It catches wind currents without flapping, maintaining its course and preserving its energy. The Seagull symbolizes personal freedom, a carefree attitude, and calmness.

I am a Seagull. I feel a sense of freedom and harmony with Nature. I am a work in progress, growing and developing positively each day, constantly moving forward. I pause and keep the awareness of the natural synchronicity of life's daily occurrences. There are no coincidences in Mother Nature.

I remember the Seagull. I am resourceful and intelligent. I trust my abilities and am equipped for challenges and difficult situations that arise during my day. When I feel exhausted or drained, I catch the wind current of Mother Nature to uplift me. I know that She is always there for me at any time I care to reach out for love and support.

TODAY:
I am gentle with myself and others. I love myself. I am free.

Source: U.S. Fish & Wildlife Service

I am a Wolf

———⟨⟨∾⟩⟩———

*A*lthough the Wolf is feared, it is respectable, faithful, tough, and very protective of its offspring. The Wolf is not typically a loner; it travels in packs of its nuclear family. The Wolf is a leader and is linked to the concept of free will because of its ability to escape.

I am a Wolf. I have choices each day. Physically and figuratively, I can show up and be present, or I can abandon myself and others. I can be a lone wolf or I can be social and enjoy my relationships. Although I allow myself quiet time alone, I also connect with Mother Earth and other living beings to recharge. At times, I may feel like isolating myself from others, but I am also a faithful companion to Mother Earth, myself, and others. I realize that if I escape, I will be missed.

I remember the Wolf. I am a leader in certain circumstances and also part of the pack. I value myself, but I am also loyal to my social and natural environment. I respect others and possess respect for myself.

TODAY:
I am the leader of my life. I love myself. I am loyal to Mother Earth.

Source: Takkk

I am a Rainbow

The Rainbow commonly conveys a sense of childlike wonder and natural curiosity because it is such an amazing and beautiful phenomenon. It symbolizes cheerfulness, joy, hope, optimism, and awakening to enlightenment. The Rainbow reflects an array of colors associated with diversity, inclusiveness, cooperation, and promise.

I am a Rainbow. I reflect my characteristics through showing my true colors. After a personal storm, I awaken with optimism and celebrate a new beginning. I appreciate diversity and cooperate with Mother Earth. My colorful self flows and I depend on Mother Earth as She creates natural miracles in my life.

I remember the Rainbow. When it feels dark and cold from life's Rain of turbulence, I always stay hopeful because of the promise of a new colorful day. Both the Rainbow and I are examples of Mother Nature's creative magnificence.

TODAY:
I am a child of Mother Earth. I love myself. I accept and embrace Nature's natural rhythms in my life.

Source: Nasa.gov

I am the Wind

———— *ornamental divider* ————

The Wind is a source of energy that can be soft or powerful, but is always full of grace. Although invisible, we know the Wind exists; its movement of air powers sails, hot air balloons, kites, and hang gliders. The Wind also aids plants and immobile organisms in their dispersal of seeds and pollen.

I am the Wind. I am everlasting. My physical body exists at this moment but I recognize that when I become invisible, my soul still exists. I am strong like a gust of Wind but can also be like a cool breeze and more subtle in my actions. I am a source of positive energy. My true self, the intangible that lies inside, is my brilliance, my beauty, and my gift to Mother Earth. I share these gifts with others.

I remember the Wind. I am a powerful force of Nature. I am eternal. My higher self is my true being. I see the beauty of my inner self. Just like the Wind, my beauty, strength, humility, and grace are invisible.

TODAY:
I am graceful. I love myself. I recognize my true worth.

Source: Shredex

I am Lightning

—⁓⦿⟞⦿⟝⦿⁓—

$\mathscr{L}$ightning is intimidating, powerful, inspiring, and dangerous. It is always accompanied by thunder and rarely strikes twice in the same place. Lightning also warns us that a storm is near. Lightning is associated with new ideas and inspiration but is also a symbol for repressed emotions and the need to express oneself.

I am Lightning. At times I feel unbalanced, experiencing both positive and negative emotions together. Yet, I constructively express myself in a variety of forms to relieve me of these internal stresses. I write, exercise, meditate, and create. I either share with others or simply connect with Mother Nature. I am spectacular like Lightning and often have breakthroughs of creativity and awareness. Just as Lightning typically does not strike twice, I learn from my mistakes in order to avoid duplicating poor choices and unhealthy habits. I don't allow negative energy and experiences to hinder my path.

I remember Lightning. Through expressive actions, I discharge feelings of self-doubt, self-pity, resentment, self-centeredness, self-seeking, and grandiosity. I initiate change in my life by recognizing truth through sudden, subtle realizations. I have strength each day because I am connected to Mother Earth, like Lightning is to thunder. I have faith and walk through my fears.

TODAY:
I am balanced. I love myself. I focus on the positive.

Source: <u>M. Klüber Fotografie</u>

I am a Bull

---~~m~~oeros~~oues~~ow---

$\mathscr{T}$he Bull is aggressive, stubborn, unpredictable, dangerous, and forceful. The Bull represents perseverance, passion, determination, liveliness, and abundance. In the stock market, the Bull symbolizes an upward trend.

I am a Bull. I am responsible for my daily actions. At times I may act "Bull-headed" or strong willed because I am passionate about a subject or determined to get results to feel fulfilled. This characteristic is sometimes useful and serves me well. However, I am aware that stepping back from any extreme behavior creates a sense of balance that supports my well-being. I am a Bull so I gracefully charge through obstacles.

I remember the Bull. I am lively, truthful, confident, passionate, and possess determination. I work hard in order to create positive outcomes in my life. I also knowingly connect with Mother Earth, who supports my opportunities for abundance, wealth, and success.

TODAY:
I persevere. I love myself. I am fulfilled.

Source: Newlitter

I am a Horse

The Horse is strong in stature, speedy, agile, sensitive, and grounded. Its strong sense of balance, highly developed vision, and sensitivity to touch gives the horse the ability to instinctively connect with its body. The Horse moves at a natural pace but possesses the ability to trot and gallop. It responds well to a consistent routine. A spirited animal with a calm temperament, the Horse is an emblem for freedom and also represents strong motivation carried through life.

I am a Horse. I am aware of my surroundings at all times. I see the beauty in life's simplicity. I am physically and mentally grounded exactly where my feet are planted at this moment. I trust in my inner strength and patience, and I appreciate my powerful senses as a strong life-force of Mother Earth. Just as the Horse requires regular grooming, hoof care, vaccinations, and dental exams, I also practice self-care and take pride in my physical, emotional, and spiritual maintenance.

I remember the Horse. I am alert, spirited, bold, and free. I am motivated to develop through my journey in order to connect with my purpose. I move naturally through the course of my life. I honor my path.

TODAY:
I am healthy. I love myself. I am sensitive
to my inner strength and spirit.

Source: Agreene12

I am a Waterfall

———∿∽᙮◦᙮◦᙮◦᙮∾∿———

There are various types of Waterfalls. Large Waterfalls flow powerfully and are a vision of the phenomenon of Mother Earth. Small Waterfalls also exist, possessing a soothing sound to our ears.

I am a Waterfall. I complement my surroundings just as the Waterfall naturally complements Mother Earth's upward climb of rocks. The Waterfall is renewed each second, just as I have opportunities to cleanse myself of negative emotions and to create a fresh start throughout my day. I let go of limited beliefs and frustrations. I completely rejuvenate by calming my body, mind, and soul through healing modalities, such as prayer, stretching, meditation, walking, surrounding myself with Mother Nature, and listening to tranquil music. I discover the path that is fitting for me.

I remember the Waterfall. As I continue through my day, I am aware of my ability to pause, let go, and take a few cleansing breaths to clear and calm my soul. I flow consistently throughout my day no matter what challenges I may encounter.

TODAY:
I complement Mother Nature. I love myself. I am rejuvenated.

Source: Jose Maria Plazaola

I am the Snow

—⌇⌇⌇⌇⌇⌇⌇—

Snowflakes vary in size and shape, creating intricate and
unique structures. The Snow is a seasonal image representing
individuality, peace, tranquility, and purity. Due to its slow and soft
falling nature, it is also associated with gentleness and serenity.

I am the Snow. Like each Snowflake, I consist of many unique
characteristics which make up my individual personality. There
is no one else exactly like me. Just as the Snowflake crystals
form one compact structure, I am independent and unique
but also a part of Mother Earth. I am pure. No matter what
actions I have taken or words I have spoken in the past, I remind
myself that today the impurities in my life are dismissed. I
forgive myself of past mistakes and poor judgment and I gently
begin my day whole and clean of prior destructive feelings.

I remember the Snow. I am individual, unlike any other.
Although I am unique, I recognize that I share similar feelings,
capabilities, and experiences with my fellow Snowflakes.
I am not alone. I have peace and serenity throughout my
day because I choose to keep my heart and soul pure.

TODAY:
I am gentle with myself. I love myself. I am cleansed.

Source: We-El

I am the Soil

—⦿⦿⦿⦿⦿⦿—

Soil is a natural mixture of multiple solids and gases. Often called "dirt," soil is the home of many microscopic organisms. It is a source of food for plants and insects. Soil is always changing due to shifting conditions. Soil represents the concepts of opportunity, growth, and fertility.

I am the Soil. I am grounded on Earth. I am a mixture of characteristics, experiences, and talents. If I align myself with my Source, Mother Nature, I grow when opportunities present themselves, just as plants and flowers grow from the Soil. I use challenges and hardships as growth opportunities to develop my character. Also, Mother Earth simply blesses me with little buds of miracles.

I remember the Soil. The Soil accepts its diverse consistency. It is nurtured by Mother Earth and creates a stable environment for natural, abundant opportunity. I must care for myself in the same way as the Soil must be tended. If I nurture myself and possess a positive attitude, I will cultivate a variety of abundance in my life.

TODAY:
I have opportunities. I love myself. I am abundant.

Source: Wildfeuer

I am a Leaf

———⚬⚬⚬⚬⚬———

Leaves come in all shapes, structures, and sizes. Leaves are adaptive and seasonal; they change color when they experience cold and reduced sunlight and eventually fall and die. The common phrase, "Turning over a new Leaf," is symbolic for a chance at a new start and making amends for past mistakes.

I am a Leaf. Just as the Leaf is part of the plant or tree, I am one of many living beings that exist in Mother Nature. I have unique physical traits that include my look, shape, and size, and also my own personal characteristics. I embrace all aspects of myself. I may change color as a leaf does throughout the seasonal shifts, but my inside essence remains the same. Even when I feel drained, stressed, or exhausted and not connected to my inner self or Mother Earth, my true essence is always present. I just need to pause and take a few deep breaths to get perspective. I am always one with Nature.

I remember the Leaf. Although I am unique, I am part of the whole. I always have a chance to create a new beginning. I embrace all the seasons of my life. I am beautiful. I focus on the beauty that lies within me and radiates outward. I was created in the image of Mother Earth.

TODAY:

I am new. I love myself. I am beauty.

Source: Charlesjsharp

I am a Butterfly

The Butterfly is a bright colored species that flutters gracefully. It experiences four life cycles: the egg, larvae (caterpillar), pupa (cocoon), and adult. The entire life cycle only lasts about a month. Butterflies are commonly associated with massive transformation, inevitable change, and rebirth. The Butterfly has also been known as a symbol of the soul.

I am a Butterfly. I experience cycles of life that include growing pains, times of weakness, and also moments of major positive development. The metamorphosis of the Butterfly parallels my soul's journey; I keep faith as I undergo transitions in my life. The journey has turns, shifts, and conditions which cause me to morph into a greater being. I will brilliantly emerge just as the Butterfly from its cocoon to become graceful, beautiful, and bright. I recognize that some transitions work rapidly while others require patience. I pause and appreciate the journey.

I remember the Butterfly. The Butterfly signifies time, growth, surrender, and the vulnerability of life's essential path. Transition is connected to transformation, which I must ultimately surrender to daily. Life is dynamic and ever-changing; the only guarantee is the journey. I remain positive, patient, and open to a glorified life of progress as I cycle through my life's phases.

TODAY:

I practice progress. I love myself. I am patient through transformation.

Source: Luke Elstad

I am an Ant

———∿∽∘◦⊙◦∘∽∿———

An Ant is a social insect. Despite their tiny size, ants are "workers" or "soldiers" and operate as a unified entity. They work collectively to support their colony. Ants symbolize hard work, diligence, cooperation, structure, order, strength, and patience.

I am an Ant. I accept my role. I practice self-care and care of others, not self-centeredness, and work with others to support Mother Nature. I plan and organize my day while cooperating with Mother Earth. I may have as strong a will as the Ant, but I do not force events to happen. I can only control myself and my actions, not any other being of Nature. I persevere because I know that all good things come with time and effort.

I remember the Ant. I may seem miniature, but my work ethic, self-discipline, and endurance make me a strong, willful soldier of Mother Earth. I accept and open to Her grace. Because I am not the commander of Mother Earth, I am peaceful knowing that I can take action steps only in my life, while trusting that other Ants in my colony will do the same.

TODAY:
I am responsible for myself. I love myself. I am united with Mother Earth.

Source: Phil Sangwell

I am a Rabbit

———∿∽◦⦿◦∽∿———

A Rabbit's long ears enable it to have supreme hearing. Rabbits are highly social and affectionate. They hop, jump, and leap, and also love to chew. Symbolically, Rabbits are associated with the spring season, innocence, luck, reproduction, and longevity.

I am a Rabbit. I am affectionate and loving. I lend my ears to others and hear them out, especially during the intense, anxious, and sad times. I do not interrupt. I am gentle with others just as I am with myself. If I make a mistake or poor choice, I use it as a learning experience. I, therefore, realize that failure is part of my success. I also know that the formula for success includes the practice of self-discipline, which is not deprivation or punishment. It is one of the most loving actions I can take. I embrace repetition in my daily tasks just as the Rabbit enjoys repetitive chewing.

I remember the Rabbit. I use my natural talents, learned skills, intuition, and Mother Nature to guide me through my journey. Mother Nature is constantly showing me signs of which direction to turn. I am open to all possibilities and willing to listen with my ears wide open, just as the Rabbit.

TODAY:

I am a success. I love myself. I pause and learn through listening.

Source: Kerem Barut

I am a Mountain

---ᴡᴏᴏᴇᴛᴏᴏᴇᴏᴏᴡ---

Mountains stand tall, rising above the Earth's surface. They possess different climates, elevation, and steepness. Mountains are linked with the concepts of overcoming obstacles and making progress. The Mountain's peak represents having a better perspective. Mountains symbolize constancy, eternity, and stillness.

I am a Mountain. I rise against challenges in my life. I have a positive attitude and consider myself a work in progress. I improve daily by making subtle changes, knowing that I will eventually see mountainous results. I understand that as the Mountain erodes and gets smoother over time, my rugged character flaws also get polished and I grow into the best version of myself. I am never a finished product; I am a work in progress. I am always improving, learning, and standing tall through the process.

I remember the Mountain. I am eternal. I may exist in different forms as rugged, smooth, and eventually eroded, but I still exist at all times with Mother Earth. I have prominent features that distinguish me from other elements of Mother Nature. I will always be remembered as I create my legacy.

TODAY:

I matter. I love myself. I am distinctive.

Source: MarcusObal

I am Fire

—⁓∘⊙⋅⊙⋅⊙⊙⋅∘⁓—

Fire gives off heat and light. Although commonly recognized as a negative phenomenon of Nature, Fire is an important process that stimulates growth and maintains various ecosystems. Fire allows human beings to cook, heat, and signal. It is associated with anger, passion, chaos, war, energy, connectivity, and determination.

I am Fire. I have my days of frustration, anger, and chaos. I may even feel out of control. But just as Fire, the feelings can be tamed. I know these feelings are temporary. I take actions to pause, take deep breaths, and connect with Mother Earth. I re-establish myself. Mother Earth is my anchor if I allow Her to be. As Fire, I have strong emotions, passion, and determination, but I conserve my energy throughout the day. I utilize my Energy Source when required. I strive for balance.

I remember Fire. My ability to spark a flame of ideas or share positive energy is a gift I share with others. If I fire up and create chaos, I slow down and get perspective. I lighten up to handle all situations with the help of Mother Earth.

TODAY:
I am energetic. I love myself. I am passionate.

Source: Edith Schreurs

I am a Whale

―――⳥⳥⳥⳥⳥―――

The Whale is Ruler of the Ocean who moves easily through water, yet it still breathes air. With its fins, tail, and acrobatic ability to jump high out of the water and even twirl around, the Whale is a miraculous vision. It is a symbol of emotional depth and creativity. The Whale is also associated with a nurturing nature, therefore, the natural inclination for helping others.

I am a Whale. I have deep feelings which I effectively communicate, expressing myself through speaking, writing, dancing, singing, producing visual artwork, exercising, brainstorming, gardening, and working with my hands. I embrace my creativity, which is a product of my emotional and spiritual connection to Mother Nature. This is a reciprocal relationship; I inspire and create just as Mother Nature does in return.

I remember the Whale. I am a master of navigation. I move through my emotions just as the Whale travels through water. I may have uneasy feelings or unfavorable experiences, but I recognize that these are temporary and I will grow and learn from them.

TODAY:
I am expressive. I love myself. I create and embrace various forms of expression.

I am a Tornado

———⟶ ᨄᨆᨆᨆᨆᨆᨆ ———

The Tornado is a violently rotating column of air in contact with the ground and is frequently called a twister or cyclone. The Tornado is Earth's most powerful storm with the strongest winds of all. It is a dangerous phenomenon, but a Tornado usually only lasts a few minutes. It is the master change maker, a symbol for awakening and a metaphor for social change.

I am a Tornado. Sometimes life situations cause me to spiral out of control and feel overwhelmed. I have chaotic thoughts when I am about to face a challenge, which create feelings of anxiety. However, I trust that it will pass, just as the Tornado eventually passes through.

I remember the Tornado. I experience transformation and an awakening through the challenges and situations that place me out of my comfort zone. When life is stressful and I feel I am lacking control, I honor Mother Earth. I have faith that these times are temporary and if I move forward each day, they will pass. I accept that many facets of my life are not in my control, so I let go.

TODAY:
I am awakened. I love myself. I embrace change.

I am Mother Earth

———⟡———

*M*other Earth is the life-giving Force and the Sustainer of life. She nurtures all aspects of the world. Mother Earth smells the flowers, speaks with the animals, listens to the wind and rain, feels the soil, and fosters the beauty of all that exists. She is the personification of Nature, reminding us that we are never alone.

When I feel connected to the natural world, emotional healing and spiritual awakening occur. I humbly recognize that my body is a temporary home whose health is necessary for my spirit. Nature is life and life is body, mind, and spirit.

I remember Mother Earth. I turn to Her in times of need. She is my safety net, my creativity, my intuition, and my foundation for all answers.

TODAY:
I am Mother Earth. I love myself. I am healed and protected.

CPSIA information can be obtained
at www.ICGtesting.com
Printed in the USA
FFOW03n1832120417
34478FF